140 GREAT FASHION DESIGNS

1950-2000

CD-ROM AND BOOK

DOVER PUBLICATIONS INC.
MINEOLA, NEW YORK

The CD-ROM in this book contains all of the images. Each image has been scanned at 300 dpi and saved in TIFF format. There is no installation necessary. Just insert the CD into your computer and call the images into your favorite software (refer to the documentation with your software for further instructions).

All of the graphics files are in the Images folder on the CD. Every image has a unique file name in the following format: xxx.TIF. The first 3 digits of the file name correspond to the number printed under the image in the book. The last 3 letters of the file name, "TIF," refer to the file format. So, 001.TIF would be the first file in the Images folder.

Also included on the CD-ROM is Dover Design Manager, a simple graphics editing program for Windows that will allow you to view, print, crop, and rotate the images.

For technical support, contact:
Telephone: 1 (617) 249-0245
Fax: 1 (617) 249-0245
Email: dover@artimaging.com
Internet: **http://www.dovertechsupport.com**
The fastest way to receive technical support is via email or the Internet.

FIVE DECADES OF FASHION
1950–2000

During the fifties, Christian Dior continued as the most powerful influence in haute couture, yet the world of fashion would see increasingly rapid changes of style. Although Paris still held unquestioned fashion leadership, the primary target of every design house became the American marketplace, and in America the media were beginning to gobble up and demand more and more fashions. Growing numbers of television viewers, now accustomed to seeing stars like Faye Emerson and Loretta Young weekly sporting the latest fashions, wanted more. Dior's response was to create a new "line" as soon as he felt the sales of the past season were in danger of dropping. In 1950 his traditional "new look" was recut emphasizing the diagonal to give the so-called oblique line; until his death, in 1957, Dior continued to produce a succession of new "lines." Another device suited to the American marketplace was changing the height of the hemline with each new season, thus rendering last year's wardrobe visibly obsolete. Other designers soon adopted these techniques, and the erratic fashions of the fifties were the result.

Perhaps the greatest fashion news of the decade was the triumphal return, in 1954, of Coco Chanel, in retirement since the beginning of World War II. Her special brilliance lay in the fact that, in contrast to Dior, she established a "look" and a "line" with her basic suit that would change but little except in detail and material, thus giving the harried, fashion-tossed woman of the fifties a haven of elegant stability. Chanel provided an alternative to the quickening pace of change.

During the course of the decade, many of the great names of the past in design—Molyneux, Piguet, Lelong, Schiaparelli, Rochas, Fath—died or retired. As their influence waned, new commercial forces began to "democratize" couture, making it more competitive and more diverse, and accelerating the process of rapid turnovers of style. Couturiers began to manufacture their own copies in bulk and to make distribution arrangements with stores, giving exclusive rights to their designs. Hardy Amies opened his "boutique" in 1950, starting a trend that spread like wildfire.

Finally, there arose newer, youth-oriented styles. In 1955 Mary Quant opened her first Bazaar Shop in King's Row in London, espousing the "Chelsea look" with its long stockings, shorts, bottom-hugging skirts, duffle coats, and long, uncoifed hair. A fashion time bomb had begun ticking and was to explode in the next decade.

THE SIXTIES

In 1960, the reins of the high-fashion industry were still in the hands of French couturiers such as Yves Saint Laurent (for the House of Dior) and Balenciaga. But change was in the wind. During the fifties fashion had begun to go international, notable designers from Italy, Spain, Ireland, and America having made incursions into what had been a Parisian monopoly. Almost single-handedly, Mary Quant, a young Englishwoman, wrested the dictates of fashion from the Parisian designers and revolutionized the entire industry when she began to design clothes specifically for the teenager. Her clothes were notable for their bright, bold colors, short miniskirts, colorful tights in lieu of stockings and "kooky" accessories, such as thigh-high boots, wide belts and outsized shoulder bags. Her clothes were all ready-to-wear and inexpensive, leading to the concept of "throw-away" fashion. By the mid-sixties her fashion had crystallized the youth cult and had made "Swinging London" the leading center for new women's fashions. For the first time in fashion history, the designers had to cope with the reality that fashion would no longer be dictated by the elite wealthy class; the big bucks now lay in young middle- and working-class consumers who wanted comfort and flash in their ready-made clothing.

Two young Parisian designers, Courrèges and Cardin, were among the first to recognize the power of this youth cult and to formulate it as couturier fashion. Courrèges was able to corral the trends of the iconoclastic youth cult into a more formalized high fashion and was the first of the Parisian designers to raise skirts to the rarefied heights of the mini. His clothes were noted for their structured, austere, sculptured look. Cardin's contribution to the fashions of the sixties was an almost architectural look, with a clean, severe line and geometric shapes.

By the mid-sixties, the rule in fashion design was to break the rules. The most important fashion trend was the shortness of the skirt to the hip and the emphasis of the leg and novelty tights. By 1967, all designer collections seemed to feature unisex clothing—a misnomer in that it promoted women's clothing that was mannish, but did not dare to encourage men to wear dresses, although the shoulder bag was promoted as an accessory and the use of cologne and jewelry became more popular.

During the entire decade, Yves Saint Laurent was one of the decade's leading iconoclasts. Among his contributions were Pop Art fashions, see-through dresses and blouses designed to be worn over nothing at all, Mondrian-inspired geometric sheath dresses and, by the end of the decade, the introduction of the "maxi" or long skirt.

Throughout the sixties the trend was toward a more experimental, inventive and childlike appearance veneering a foundation of blatant sexuality. Couturier collections diminished to small private affairs, the emphasis shifting to the ready-to-wear business.

THE SEVENTIES

The emphasis on youth that had begun in the sixties continued into the seventies. The early seventies were a period of throwaway elegance, based on inexpensive and elaborate synthetic fabrics. There was an almost barbaric splendor in the use of silver and gold and lush textures and colors. A worldwide oil shortage beginning about 1973, and the consequent skyrocketing prices, would soon bring such extravagance to an end. At about the same time, awareness of the environmental problems of the world began to come to the fore. International concern about endangered species of animals made it socially unacceptable in many circles to wear exotic furs, and synthetic "fun" furs were promoted as an alternative.

Cheap travel and global communication suggested all sorts of exotic fashions from around the world. Mid-seventies fashion also mirrored contemporary history from space travel to Olympic events. Fabric texture or print was often substituted for cut, a trend encouraged by the explosion of designer ready-to-wear and the advent of the boutique. Saint Laurent was probably the leading designer of the decade, and led the pack in exploiting old films, exotic locations, and history to create looks for each season.

Fashion had passed from the haute couture to the mass market, a market dominated by the young who had money for clothing and few other commitments for their wages. Casual dressing became a big factor in fashion. Women were exhorted to "do their own thing," regardless of the consequences, with designers turning out fashions in deliberately bad taste. Nostalgia was a recurring theme throughout the decade, often tied into the blockbuster film of the season, as in the case of *The Great Gatsby* and the resulting revival of twenties' fashions. In 1975, the "Big Look" came into fashion, with the designer Kenzo stating, "Much too big is the right size."

The heyday of "Punk" was 1976 to 1978. Originally from the streets, punk fashions, with their rebellious, sado-masochistic overtones and concentration on the outrageous, were associated with underground music. Punk-rock stars sported black rubber dresses, oversize crosses, Nazi memorabilia, spike-heeled shoes and spiky hairdos, black leather corsetry, death-symbolism accessories and caked, geometric makeup. In response, fashion collections went black and bits and pieces of punk fashions were incorporated.

Middle Eastern and folk costume also became the inspiration for 1976 fashion, bringing tunics, turbans, capes and hoods. By 1978, designers had turned the street look of punk into the "New Romanticism" with modern versions of ruffles, crinolines, flounces, ribbons and bows, deep décolleté, mock bustles, and leg-o'-mutton sleeves, all with a purposely disheveled look to the hair, heavy makeup and gaudy costume jewelry. By the end of the seventies there seemed to be no particular direction to fashion, each designer pursuing his or her own inspiration and offering his or her own look.

THE EIGHTIES

The fashion designers of the 1980s, like many of their predecessors of the late 1970s, found inspiration in the designs of the past. The real news of this decade was in ease of wear and fit. Comfort became key; no longer would women be constricted and confined by structured foundation garments.

With the unusually cold winter weather of the early 1980s came a drop in hemlines and a layering of outerwear. When winters warmed in the second half of the decade, skirt lengths rose and outerwear became lighter, too.

In fabrics, polyester was "out" and natural fabrics were "in." The type and style of fabric—luxury fabrics, novelty weaves, and prints—often became more important than the cut of the clothing.

During the eighties, the split widened between high fashion and mass fashion. Men and women who were obsessed with fitness and running inspired those less active to wear jogging suits, stretch body suits, gym shorts, tee shirts, and running shoes for leisure. While some women continued to choose dresses for office, cocktails, and evening wear, more and more women preferred the comfort and convenience of pants.

With the 1980s came a great demand in the mass market for "designer label ready-to-wear." As a result, more clothing designers rose to prominence during the eighties than in any previous decade.

THE NINETIES

The fashions of the last decade of the 20th century were as volatile as the weather. In the search for new styles, the fashion industry lurched from "modern" to "retro," from "grunge" to "glamour," from "glitz" to "minimalist" to "military," concluding in a flurry of sumptuous beaded, jeweled, and embroidered garments. The decade also was marked by mega-mergers of design houses and the blurring of product lines—for example, producers of luggage turned to fashion design to enter new markets. In an attempt to revitalize old couture houses, "hot" young designers hopped from house to house. To add to the confusion, some designers had their own label but also designed for another establishment, such as Michael Kors for Celine, John Galliano for Dior, Alexander McQueen for Givenchy, and Marc Jacobs for Perry Ellis. By the end of the 1990s, supermodels were losing ground as fashion oracles as they were replaced by rock stars and entertainment personalities.

NOTES ON THE DESIGNS

001. **1950, Dior Oblique-line evening dress.**

002. **1951, Norman Norell wasp-waisted dress.** This dress features a small flyaway bolero and is worn over a butterfly-bow silk blouse.

003. **1951, Jacques Heim pants and blouse.** Wrapped bottle-green jersey blouse, tapered blue-green velvet pants, and lilac cummerbund.

004. **1951, Mainbocher cotton dress.** Cotton petticoat "cracked open" at neck and skirt, white organdie collar and skirt, which was worn over a crinoline half-slip.

005. **1952, Fath bell suit.** This navy blue wool suit has a plunging neckline with a massive bouquet of silk roses and is worn over a red and white ribbon silk collar and bow; the suit is nipped in at the waist, with a padded bell hipline.

006. **1952, Sybil Connolly pullover blouse and at-home skirt.** Blouse is of white crochet and features a deep V-neckline and scalloped edging on sleeves and waist.

007. **1952, Balenciaga plaid suit.** Suit made of wine-and-white wool plaid; waist is around the hips. White silk scarf, wine hat, gloves, and shoes.

008. **1953, Hardy Amies evening gown.** Silk with a fitted bodice and full skirt of tiny pleats, worn with a full-length stole.

009. **1953, Elspeth Champcommunal (for Worth) white lace gown.** Designed in the year of Queen Elizabeth's coronation, this gown features stand-up lace panels, flared cap sleeves, and a draped panel on one side of the full skirt, whose fullness to the back suggests a train.

010. **1953, Claire McCardell "stringbean" chemise with matching "shortie" jacket.** Chemise could be worn with a cummerbund or hung straight.

011. **1954, Dior H-line suit.** Plum-colored wool with matching accessories.

012. **1954, Chanel jersey suit.** Designed at the time of Chanel's return to the world of fashion, this suit features squared shoulders and a tucked white blouse, with a bow tie and a sailor's hat tipped to the back of the head.

013. **1954, Balmain ball gown.** Pink satin with cotton lace floral design appliqué, fuchsia-colored gloves and fan.

014. **1955, Dior A-line suit.** Honey beige raw silk; features a flared tunic-length jacket and box-pleated skirt worn with a flowerpot hat.

015. **1955, Pauline Trigère evening dress.** Made of peau-de-soie fabric.

016. **1955, Pertegaz evening coat.** Emerald paper-taffeta evening coat in tiers, worn over a sheer lace short evening dress; dyed-to-match satin shoes.

017. **1956, Balenciaga sack-back day dress.** Tobacco-brown wool jersey dress features a huge cowl collar and extremely dropped waist, winter white molded helmet and rust-colored suede cloth gloves.

018. **1956, Dior evening dress.** Blue silk taffeta flat-bosomed evening dress with skirt puffing from the hips; worn over stiffened crinoline petticoats.

019. **1956, Charles James opera coat.** Black velvet with a puffed, gathered, dropped hipline ending in a trumpet-flared skirt; an oversize red silk poppy is worn to the side and back of the rounded stand-up collar.

020. **1957, Givenchy sack dress.** Pink wool jersey with red silk bow, red jersey turban, red gauntlet gloves, black straw handbag, and black leather shoes.

021. **1957, Yves Saint Laurent (for Dior) trapeze-line wedding dress.** From Saint-Laurent's first collection for the house of Dior.

022. **1957, Dior wool coat.** A barrel-shaped coat, almost a cape, with huge sleeves; worn with a veiled flowerpot hat.

023. **1958, Chanel jersey suit.** This suit is hung with gold chains.

024. **1958, Cardin suit with blouse-backed jacket.** Made of black-and-white hound's-tooth-checked men's wool suiting. Worn with a white straw flowerpot hat, white gloves, and black patent-leather shoes.

025. **1958, Madame Grès evening dress.** Short black taffeta sheath with two shades of blue taffeta draped over the front, creating a halter neckline and ending in a pouf at the hem.

026. **1959, Yves Saint Laurent evening suit.** Ruby red surah silk with jacket ending in a gathered pouf over a skirt that repeats the pouf; sculptured hairdo and matching red accessories.

027. **1959, Irene Galitzine sheath dress.** White satin sheath overlaid with silver-studded sheer fabric; gathered froufrou stole doubles as a long skirt.

028. **1959, Givenchy gold-lamé dress with cuffed skirt.** Beaded gold lamé worn with diamond choker necklace and bracelet; full-length white gloves; stiffly lacquered, sculptured hairdo.

029. **1960, House of Dior black-and-white silk print suit.** Worn with a straw beehive hat.

030. **1960, Jacques Heim cotton evening dress.** The full skirt is ankle-length in front, floor-length in back; contrasting bow and band ornamentation.

031. **1960, Yves Saint Laurent transparent chiffon dress.** Bands of beading; flesh-colored underwear.

032. **1961, Irene Galitzine crepe jacket and sheath.** Bias-scarfed combing jacket; jeweled at the neckline.

033. **1961, Jacques Griffe linen suit.** Worn with a straw flowerpot hat.

034. **1962, Pierre Balmain evening gown.** Long, paneled dress reminiscent of the nineteenth century. The bodice is embroidered with gold and coral paillettes and has bare shoulders.

035. **1962, Capucci chiffon cape-and-sheath outfit.** Open-front cape with rounded back; severe casquelike hat.

036. **1962, Courrèges nine-tenths coat.** Worn with a leather hat.

037. **1963, Yves Saint Laurent organdy outfit.** Silk, with guipure lace.

038. **1963, Jean Patou organdy gown.** Embroidered, with appliquéd motifs.

039. **1963, Givenchy tweed sport suit.**

040. **1964, Chanel nubby-weave suit.** Straight-cut skirt and hip-length box jacket; a gardenia tops the straw hat.

041. **1964, Larry Aldrich unwaisted crepe dress with stole.** Bianchini rayon crepe; a kick-pleat flips out at the hem. Straw hat by Halston.

042. **1964, Courrèges jersey pants and jacket.** The pants are slit at the ankle over leather boots; pearl-buttoned jacket; "waste basket" hat.

043. **1965, Yves Saint-Laurent jersey day dress.** Patterning in the manner of Mondrian.

044. **1965, Pucci minidress.** Pucci print worn over tights; artificial braids create fantastic hairdo.

045. **1965, Courrèges wool coat-dress.** Twill bound with grosgrain ribbon; shovel hat.

046. **1966, Paco Rabanne plastic dress.** Gilded plastic rectangles joined by metal links.

047. **1966, Courrèges whipcord and organza jumpsuit.** Worn over flesh-colored underpants.

048. **1967, Mary Quant wool minidress.** Industrial zipper down the front; felt helmet with nylon braids.

049. **1967, Rudi Gernreich silk dress.** Loose, straight line; full dolman sleeves.

050. **1967, Bill Blass crepe wedding dress.** Silk crepe with coat with jewel buttons; ice-white stripes and scallops.

051. **1968, Oscar de la Renta organdy overblouse and shorts.** Floral appliqué (flowers punched and appliquéd with silver center); elasticized jersey shoe stockings by David Evins.

052. **1968, Geoffrey Beene coat-dress.**

053. **1968, Anne Fogarty "little girl" dress.** Wig inspired by Little Orphan Annie.

054. **1969, Courrèges dress.** Curved dress with a carved-out V neckline.

055. **1969, Pierre Cardin wool coat, hooded sweater, and white skirt.** Coat falling to the instep, rimmed with black cording; ribbed sweater belted into short skirt.

056. **1969, Yves Saint Laurent evening dress.** Patchwork skirt of satin squares; blouse and scarf of sheer print.

057. **1970, Yves Saint Laurent lamé dress.** One of Saint Laurent's lamé "hooker" dresses.

058. **1970, House of Dior crepe-de-chine dress.** Dress with long georgette sleeves is topped by a floor-length sheer sheath and worn with a tasseled turban and feather fan.

059. **1970, Zandra Rhodes quilted satin dress.** Dress has a snakeskin choker hung with knotted suede strips. Worn with a fringed shawl and knee-high suede boots.

060. **1971, Tuffin and Foale checkerboard-print dress and quilted trousers.**

061. **1971, Biba wool pantsuit.** Plaid wool with matching tie and boy's billed cap.

062. **1971, Chloé wraparound skirt and shawl.** Two silk semicircles, one worn as a wraparound skirt, the other as a shawl; worn with a black jersey top.

063. **1972, Bill Blass pleated skirt and dropped-waist top.** Nostalgic twenties-look ensemble with a dropped-waist top over a short, pleated skirt, a monogrammed scarf and a matching cloche.

064. **1972, Mary Quant's two-piece dress.** Thirties-look polka-dot crepe-de-chine dress, worn with a crocheted turban and thick-soled sandals.

065. **1973, Ted Lapidus wool pantsuit.** This suit features a finger-length, bias-cut, flared jacket over bell-bottom trousers.

066. **1973, Yves Saint Laurent cardigan, pleated skirt and see-through blouse.** Thirties look features a wool-and-chenille velvet cardigan with an ostrich-feather collar; a pleated, wool-crepe skirt; a mousseline-de-soie blouse; and a cloche.

067. **1973, Roland Klein silk jersey dress.** Klein interprets the sensuous glamour of the thirties in a gown with tiny covered buttons down the front. The model wears a sleek turban and carries a leather envelope bag and a long faux fox-fur scarf.

068. **1974, Loris Azzaro mousseline-de-soie gown.** Azzaro's version of the "Gatsby Look," worn over a crepe undersheath pailletted in pearls and colored paste gems.

069. **1974, Laug lamé top and crepe-georgette skirt.** Thirties-inspired glamour in Laug's pleated lamé top over a pleated crepe-georgette skirt.

070. **1974, Sonia Rykiel cape, sweater, and skirt.** The cape has a ribbon-banded collar that crisscrosses the body and ties at the waist. The wool sweater, softly pleated skirt, scarf and felt slouch hat have a thirties "spy" look.

071. **1975, John Bates's duster.** This ensemble has a nipped-waisted, dolman-sleeved duster over a dirndl-skirted shirtwaist dress.

072. **1975, Laura Ashley pinafore, skirt, blouse, and apron.** Ashley turned to the era of Beatrix Potter for this pinafore worn over a cotton, floral-print, puff-sleeved blouse and a cotton pin-tucked skirt. Over the pinafore is an apron.

073. **1976, Halston shirtwaist dress and jacket.** Classic crepe-de-chine shirtwaist dress and matching Ultrasuede jacket.

074. **1976, Yves Saint Laurent "peasant-look" cape, blouse, skirt, and turban.** Billowing taffeta skirt, embroidered blouse and turban.

075. **1977, Hubert de Givenchy dinner dress with detachable sleeves.** A flowered silk-chiffon strapless dinner dress with detachable full sleeves from Givenchy's Nouvelle Boutique.

076. **1977, Sisan for Valentino coordinated blouse, skirt, pants, and scarf.** Silk blouse, tie-on skirt and full-legged pants. A matching scarf is tied into a turban.

077. **1977, Kenzo "Big Look" cotton shirt and skirt.**

078. **1978, Courrèges jacket, sweater, shirt, and trousers.** Chevron-patterned cotton jacket trimmed with velvet, pullover sweater over man's shirt and ascot, and cotton satin trousers. Worn with man-styled bluchers, a derby and a boutonniere.

079. **1978, Oscar de la Renta velvet dress.** Slinky, soft, narrow velvet dress with full-cut sleeves. The hammered brass belt is by Tess Shalom.

080. **1978, Yves Saint Laurent evening ensemble.** This Mongolian-looking evening ensemble consists of a silk-ciré hooded coat, embroidered with sequins and trimmed in mink, and satin pants trimmed with tassels, worn with mink-trimmed leather boots. Under the coat is a knitted gold jersey bodice.

081. **1979, Thierry Mugler jumpsuit.** Mugler's creations were often outrageous, but strong on basic line, as in this space-age cotton jumpsuit.

082. **1979, Claude Montana gabardine trench coat.** This coat exploits the new interest in wide shoulders.

083. **1979, Albert Capraro velvet-and-silk evening gown.** The bodice of this evening costume is of velvet trimmed with silk fringe. The shoulders and bosom are worked in jet beads and silk. The skirt is of the same ribbed silk.

084. **1979, Ralph Lauren silk smoking jacket.** Lauren redefines the classic man's smoking jacket in paisley silk trimmed in satin, putting it over a Victorian blouse and sleek trousers.

085. **1980, Betty Hanson and Company shirtwaist dress and short jacket.** Accessories include a belt, shoes, and hat with a handkerchief, and bangle bracelet.

086. **1980, Missoni jacket, hat, and scarf.** Oversized, woolen plaid jacket and hat, worn with a box-pleated skirt. The red of the plaid is picked up in the heel of the shoes.

087. **1980, Claude Montana cotton dress.** Oversized dress worn with matching trousers.

088. **1980, Halston classic sheath and box coat.**

089. **1981, Perry Ellis tank top, with skirt, petticoats, knit cap, and stockings.** The softly pleated skirt is worn over flounced petticoats. A striped knit cap and stockings complete the look.

090. **1981, Calvin Klein metallic print dress with knee-high leather boots.** Oversized dress with a plunging neckline and wide leather belt.

091. **1982, Giorgio Armani blouse with cut-off pants.** Layered blouson blouse with full cut-off pants.

092. **1982, Marc Bohan for House of Dior suit.** Bohan used black and white, a favorite Dior color theme, to create a suit with longer, narrower lines. It was accessorized with a black bow tie, earrings, gloves, and shoes.

093. **1982, Kasper silk "tee" shirt and skirt.** The top has graduated stripes and is worn over a softly gathered long skirt in the same material.

094. **1983, Bernard Perris flannel suit.** Trimmed with snakeskin. Completing the ensemble is a broad pinwheel hat and large silk scarf worn in a puff at the shoulder.

095. **1983, Carolina Herrera organza gown.** Summer gown has a fitted bodice and dirndl skirt. It was worn with a betsy, or ruff, at the neck.

096. **1983, Karl Lagerfeld for the House of Chloé dress with beads and sequins.** Luxurious dress with the image of a running faucet composed of beads and sequins. It may have been influenced by Schiaparelli's surrealist-informed designs of the '30s.

097. **1984, Bill Blass evening gown.** Heavy satin in lightning bolt colors.

098. **1984, Norma Kamali fleece top coat, slacks and brimmed hat.**

Man-styled top coat worn with matching slacks, a super-long scarf, and a brimmed hat reminiscent of a fedora.

099. **1984, Valentino silk sheath.** Evening sheath in silk jersey, the sparkling diamond clips emphasizing the squared shoulder line.

100. **1985, Donna Karan suede jacket, wool-jersey skirt, and suede boots.** Winter outfit combining a blouson jacket with broad, padded shoulders and an asymmetrical waistband, worn over a long, flared skirt and boots.

101. **1985, Gianfranco Ferré suede jacket over slacks.** Brightly colored jacket which was worn over full-cut slacks.

102. **1986, Anne Klein sweater dress with patent leather belt.** Broad shouldered sweater dress featuring broad stripes of red, white, and black.

103. **1986, Adolfo dress with a full-length zipper.**

104. **1986, Krizia ribbed cashmere and mohair sweater dress and coat.**

105. **1987, Yves Saint Laurent silk-crepe evening gown.** Evening dress with a plunging neckline, split skirt, and huge taffeta bow at the waist. It was accessorized with a cartwheel hat, long gloves, stockings, and shoes.

106. **1987, Geoffrey Beene lace confection.**

107. **1987, Oscar de la Renta short dress.** Shortened version of a '50s Dior dress with a touch of Schiaparelli's shocking pink.

108. **1988, Emanuel Ungaro strapless dress with dropped waist and short skirt.** Full, shortened skirt is caught up to the side by a huge rose.

109. **1988, Arnold Scaasi evening dress with velvet bodice and satin skirt.** Low-cut gown with dropped waistline.

110. **1988, Carolyn Roehm wool crepe dress with a bolero jacket.**

111. **1988, Christian Lacroix wool suit with mink facing.** Two-piece zippered suit worn with a black bag and shoes.

112. **1989, Bob Mackie gown in chiffon over silk with a sequin-studded jacket.** Chiffon over magenta silk, worn with a sequin-studded short jacket.

113. **1990 Emanuel Ungaro's lamé evening gown.** Simple but stunning in its cut and drape.

114. **1990, Christian Lacroix's pattern silk ensemble.** Jacket and skirt ensemble cleverly mixes different patterns of the same color.

115. **1990, Geoffrey Beene's silk jacquard evening ensemble.**

116. **1991, Oscar de la Renta silk shantung dress and coat.**

117. **1991, Valentino's bell-skirted evening ensemble.** Ensemble has sheer yoke and sleeves and bow accent.

118. **1991, Todd Oldham patchwork plaid suit.** Miniskirted suit with coordinated blouse.

119. **1992, Arnold Scaasi polka dot strapless crepe dress.**

120. **1992, Bob Mackie velvet-and-taffeta evening gown.**

121. **1992, Michael Kors short strapless dress and cardigan.** Lace-over-silk strapless dress, worn with coordinated cardigan.

122. **1993, Bill Blass knit tube dress.**

123. **1993, Adolfo polka-dot ensemble.** Adolfo's version of kabuki style in polka-dot prints, worn over matching bell bottoms.

124. **1993, Linda Allard for Ellen Tracy pin-stripe suit.** Man-tailored suit with full trousers.

125. **1994, Nina Ricci pleated silk gown.** Multi-tiered gown marks a return to glamour.

126. **1994, Louis Féraud evening gown with cape-like collar.**

127. **1994, Jean-Louis Scherrer minidress ball gown.** Scherrer combines the modern minidress with the classic ball gown in this embroidered, jeweled confection.

128. **1995, Vera Wang corset-bodice ball gown.** The name Vera Wang denotes memorable wedding dresses, but the designer is equally adept with elegant ball gowns, as displayed in this cyclamen-pink satin gown with corset-style bodice and voluminous net skirt and matching gloves.

129. **1995, Thierry Mugler miniskirted suit and vinyl pants.** Shaped, closely fitted wool miniskirted suit with flared jacket, worn over vinyl pants.

130. **1996, Donna Karan's body-hugging silk knit tube dress.**

131. **1996, Carolina Herrera satin wedding suit.** The low-cut jacket's coattails descend in a flared train.

132. **1996, Norma Kamali panne lamb-trimmed ensemble.** Velvet bolero with Mongolian lamb trim, worn over matching bell-bottom pants.

133. **1997, Giorgio Armani's unstructured great coat and full-cut pants.**

134. **1997, Isaac Mizrahi plunging-neckline tailored suit.**

135. **1997, Gianni Versace's slinky silk knit evening gown.**

136. **1998, John Galliano for Dior "Scheherazade" kimono and gown.** This ensemble combines eastern motifs with Art Deco opulence. Silk velvet kimono worked with gold thread and gems; sheath dress is of double satin.

137. **1998, Karl Lagerfeld for Chloé sequin tulle dress.**

138. **1998, Alexander McQueen for Givenchy wool coat with gray fox collar.** In spite of public protests and negative publicity, many designers continue to use fur.

139. **1999, Jean Paul Gaultier ostrich-trimmed silk gown with ostrich fan.**

140. **1999, Ralph Lauren cashmere sweater with satin ball skirt.** Evening separates combine a cropped cashmere turtleneck sweater with a dropped-waist satin ball skirt.

NOTES ON THE DESIGNERS

Adolfo Sardina (b. 1933, Havana, Cuba) apprenticed to Balenciaga and then came to New York in 1948 as a millinery designer. In 1962 he started his own millinery business in New York. Switching to apparel design, he introduced a series of knits inspired by Chanel's famous tweed suits.

Aldrich, Larry (b. 1906, New York City) trained for the law, but began a career in fashion in 1927. Many of the fashions he featured, designed by Marie McCarthy, were French fashions adapted for the American woman.

Allard, Linda (b. 1940, Akron, Ohio) studied fine arts at Kent State University. In New York, she designed for H. Gallen, who created the name "Ellen Tracy" as a vehicle to present Allard's designs for the well-dressed mainstream woman.

Amies, Hardy (b. 1909, London) began designing for Lachasse, a well-known couture house in London in 1934. In 1946 he opened his own house. One of the first to offer high-fashion ready-to-wear, he opened a boutique in 1950.

Armani, Giorgio (b. 1934, Italy) studied medicine, philosophy, and worked as an assistant buyer at an Italian department store. His first menswear collection appeared in 1974, his womenswear collection in 1975. Pioneering the unconstructed blazer, Armani clothing has an easy fit, fine tailoring, and luxurious fabrics in neutral colors.

Ashley, Laura (1926–1985). Born in Wales; started her company in 1956 as a cottage industry, producing tea towels and table napkins before turning to fashion.

Azzaro, Loris (b. 1934), taught French literature in his native Tunisia and in France before opening a shop in Paris in 1966 selling accessories and beaded evening tops. He soon became known for slinky evening wear.

Balenciaga, Cristóbal (1895–1972), born in Guetaria, Spain. Opened his house in Paris in 1937, with immediate success. He came into full bloom in the fifties, creating bold, austere, elegant fashions. The superb design, fabrication and construction of his creations made him one of the very greatest couturiers.

Balmain, Pierre (1914–1982), born in Savoie, France. He studied to be an architect but financial reverses led to a career in Parisian couture. He worked for Molyneux and Lucien Lelong (with Dior) in the thirties and opened his own establishment in 1946. Not known for innovation, his creations are quietly luxurious and his clientele the aristocrats of world society.

Bates, John (b. 1938, England) worked for Herbert Sidon, 1956–58. He became the chief designer for Jean Varon, 1961. In 1974 he launched a line using his own name.

Beene, Geoffrey (b. 1927, Haynesville, Louisiana). A medical student before studying fashion design in New York City, he joined Teal Traina in 1958. Opening his own business in 1962, he is known for his imaginative use of color and for the wearability of his clothing.

Biba. Influential London boutique opened in 1963, the brainchild of fashion illustrator and designer **Barbara Hulanicki** (b. 1938, Poland). In 1969, Biba took over an Art Deco building in Kensington High Street.

Blass, Bill (b. 1922, Fort Wayne, Indiana) started as a sketch artist in New York, served in the army in WWII, then joined Anna Miller, Ltd., in 1946. He stayed with the firm when it merged with Maurice Rentner in 1959, becoming vice president, then owner. In 1970, the firm became Bill Blass, Ltd. His womenswear designs mix exquisite menswear fabrics, patterns and textures. He has been a mentor to many young American designers.

Bohan, Marc (b. 1926). French-born Marc Bohan worked for Robert Piguet and Jean Patou before joining the House of Dior in 1958. He took over its leadership in 1960, replacing Yves Saint Laurent. Marc Bohan designs are known for soft prints, ruffles, pleats, and embroidery.

Capraro, Albert (b. 1943, United States) worked for Lily Daché and Oscar de la Renta before forming a company with Ben Shaw and Jerry Guttenberg. In 1975, he gained fame when First Lady Betty Ford chose his clothes for her spring wardrobe.

Capucci, Roberto (b. 1929, Rome). Working in Italy from the end of World War II, Capucci moved his base to Paris in 1962, but returned to Rome six years later. His work is marked by the use of nontraditional materials and experimental cut.

Cardin, Pierre (b. 1922, Venice, Italy) grew up in St.-Etienne, France. He worked with Paquin and Castillo; then helped Dior create "new look." In 1950 he opened own business, called Adam and Eve, which sold women's dresses and some accessories for men. He opened his design house in 1957. He was the first designer to present both men's and women's fashions together, sparking the unisex idea.

Champcommunal, Elspeth. All Worth family connections with the firm had ended when house was sold, 1946; Champcommunal was member of Incorporated Society of London Fashion Designers; carried on tradition of Worth name.

Chanel, Gabrielle "Coco" (1883–1971), born in Saumur, France. A dominant figure in fashion from the mid-twenties; she closed her design house at the occupation of France in 1940. At age 71 in 1954 she reopened her couture house to almost immediate success.

Chloé. Upscale French ready-to-wear house founded in 1952. The principal designers for the firm in 1971 were Karl Lagerfeld and Graziella Fontana.

Connolly, Sybil (b. 1921), born in Swansea, Wales, of Irish father and Welsh mother; grew up in Ireland. She is known for the revival of traditional Irish textiles such as handkerchief linen and Carrickmacross lace. Jacqueline Kennedy chose a Sybil Connolly dress for her official White House portrait.

Courrèges, André (b. 1923, France). After a long association with Balenciaga, he opened his own house in 1961. He was one of the leading innovators of the sixties, introducing the miniskirt and trouser suit. He closed his couture business in 1966, reopening with three different divisions, each catering to a different price group.

de la Renta, Oscar (b. 1932, Dominican Republic) worked for Balenciaga in Madrid, then moved to Paris in 1961 as assistant to Antonio de Castillo. In 1963, he went to New York to design at Elizabeth Arden. He joined Jane Derby in 1965; the firm began operating as Oscar de la Renta, Ltd. after her death. De la Renta designs are extravagantly romantic and sophisticated.

Dior, Christian (1905–1957), opened his own house in 1947, launching "new look," a world-shattering collection of luxurious fashions. After Dior's death in 1957, his place was taken by his protégé, Yves Saint Laurent, whose association with the house ended when he was drafted in 1960. Marc Bohan then directed the house.

Ellis, Perry (1940–1986). After working as a sportswear buyer, American Perry Ellis began to design for the Portfolio Division of Vera Industries in 1975. Perry Ellis Sportswear, Inc. was established in 1978; Perry Ellis Menswear in 1980. His designs were known for their youth, spirit, and natural fabrics.

Fath, Jacques (1912–1954), born in Vincennes, France. His creations were noted for dramatic, ultra-chic, and body-conscious design that emphasized tiny waist and often back-flaring skirt.

Ferré, Gianfranco (b. 1945, Italy). After early starts in architecture and jewelry and accessory design, he opened his own couture house in 1974. His fine tailoring reflects his background in architecture.

Fogarty, Anne (1919–1981), born in Pittsburgh. A former model, she became famous for her paper-doll silhouette.

Féraud, Louis (b. 1920, France). In 1955 Féraud opened a boutique in Cannes. His first great success was a dress for Brigitte Bardot. His clothing blends simple structure with graphic detailing.

Galitzine, Irene (b. ca. 1916, Russia). Her aristocratic family fled to Italy from the Russian Revolution, where she studied art. She worked for three years for the Fontana sisters, Rome, and presented her first collection, 1949.

Galliano, John (b. 1960, Spain). Inspired by Madeleine Vionnet and Paul Poiret, Galliano is the master of the bias cut.

Gaultier, Jean Paul (b. 1952, Paris). At 17 he was hired by Pierre Cardin as a design assistant. Gaultier went out on his own in 1976. His witty styles always challenge the Paris establishment.

Gernreich, Rudi (1922–1985), born in Vienna. Operating out of Los Angeles, he won renown as a pioneer of the miniskirt and the introducer of the topless bathing suit.

Givenchy, Hubert de (b. 1927, Beauvais, France) began his career at age 17 working for Jacques Fath, later moving to Piguet and Schiaparelli. He opened his own house in 1952 with a collection of inexpensive cottons, and was a smash success. His later couture was greatly influenced by his friend and master, Balenciaga. Givenchy's clothing is revered for its elegant cut, fabric and workmanship.

Grès, Madame (1903–1993). Germaine Emilie Krebs trained as a sculptor before turning her talents to fashion design. In 1931–32 she began making toiles under the name Alix Barton. She was the designer at Alix from 1934 to 1942 when the house was closed by the Germans for flaunting designs featuring the colors of the French flag. She reopened the house after the war using her married name. She was noted for superb craftsmanship and innovative, elegant designs.

Griffe, Jacques (b. 1917, France). Having spent three years with Vionnet, he became a master of construction, especially in handling the bias cut; established a boutique and ready-to-wear range.

Halston (b. 1932, United States) started as a millinery designer, working for Lily Daché and Bergdorf Goodman. Halston originated the pillbox hat made famous by Jackie Kennedy in 1961 at the Kennedy inauguration. He began designing ready-to-wear in the late sixties, opening his own firm in 1972. In 1973, he sold the business to Norton Simon.

Hanson, Betty and Company. Formed in 1976, Betty Hanson and Company was a family-run business; Hall and Steven Hanson directed the operations. With imaginative use of texture, fabric, color, and shape, their clothing was intended for "real-life" dressing.

Heim, Jacques (1899–1967), born in Paris; the son of furriers, Heim was one of the first designers to sense the coming of the youth-oriented fashion era. The house of Heim closed, 1969; later reopened by new organization that purchased name.

Herrera, Carolina (b 1939) experienced the world of high society and couture clothes growing up in Caracas, Venezuela, where she was born. She launched her first ready-to-wear collection in 1981, focusing on elegant day and eveningwear. Her chic designs drew a following that included Jacqueline Onassis, Nancy Reagan, and Caroline Kennedy.

Horrockses. British ready-to-wear firm specializing in sophisticated cotton fashions.

Hulanicki, Barbara. See Biba.

James, Charles (1907–1978), born in Cambersley, England. He opened a couture establishment in London in1928, later in Paris and New York; He is considered a "designers' designer" for unusual, daring cuts; his work greatly influenced other couturiers.

Kamali, Norma (b. 1945, New York City) studied fashion illustration at the Fashion Institute of Technology. In 1969, she and her husband, Eddie Kamali, opened a tiny shop selling British imports and her inventive designs. Moving to Madison Avenue in 1974, she designed suits and lace dresses. In 1977, divorced, she established a new boutique and company called OMO (On My Own).

Karan, Donna (b. 1948, Forest Hills, New York) is the daughter of a fashion model and a haberdasher. After attending the Parsons School of Design for two years, she left to work under Anne Klein, and after Klein's death in 1974, became co-designer with Parsons classmate Louis Dell'Olio. In 1984 she opened her own firm. Her designs offer practical, flattering wearability.

Kasper, Herbert (b. 1926). Beginning as a hat designer, in 1985 American Herbert Kasper opened a sportswear company respected for its tailored, sophisticated clothing.

Kenzo (b. 1940). Japanese-born Kenzo moved to Paris in the mid-sixties. After designing several freelance collections, he opened his first boutique, Jungle Jap, in 1970.

Klein, Anne (1923–1974), born in New York, was the founder of the Junior Sophisticates label, where she pioneered sophisticated styles for women 5'4" tall and under. In 1968 she established Anne Klein & Co. Her sportswear was well-suited to the American woman's lifestyle.

Klein, Calvin (b. 1942, United States). Calvin Klein, Ltd., established in 1968, is revered for its understated, refined, luxurious fabrics.

Klein, Roland (b. 1938, France), worked for Dior and Patou in Paris before moving to England in 1965. In London, he worked at Marcel Fenez, where he had his own label. He opened his own ready-to-wear business in 1979.

Kors, Michael (b. 1959, New York) briefly attended the Fashion Institute of Technology; he left to learn about fashion first-hand at a New York boutique. He opened his design house in 1981 and is known for his sophisticated designer sportswear.

Krizia (Kriziamaglia, a company, Italy). Founded by Mariussia Mandelli in 1952, Krizia clothing is refined and witty.

Lacroix, Christian (b. 1951, France). A museum curator before becoming a designer, he opened his own couture and ready-to-wear business in mid-1987. He has been credited with revitalizing Paris couture with his irreverent wit and imaginative designs.

Lagerfeld, Karl (b. 1939, Germany). The sole designer at Chloé in 1972, in 1984 he created his own label at Chanel, designing a sportswear collection specifically for the United States market in 1985.

Lapidus, Ted (1929, France), studied technology in Tokyo; returned to Paris in his early twenties and opened a small dressmaking house. He also designed for several ready-to-wear manufacturers.

Laug, André (b. 1932, France), worked for Nina Ricci and André Courrèges, then moved to Italy where he designed for Antonelli. He opened his own couture house in 1968 and also produced ready-to-wear.

Lauren, Ralph (b. 1939, United States), began his career in fashion retailing. In 1968, he began designing a line of menswear under the label "Polo by Ralph Lauren," then branched into women's clothing in 1971. He is known for his representation of an idealized American past in his high-quality fashions, which exude an air of privileged luxury; the design shown here is a departure from typical Lauren styles.

Mackie, Bob was born in Los Angeles in 1940. He studied art and theater design and worked as a sketcher for film designers such as Edith Head. In 1969 he opened his own salon and made a splash with glamorous ready-to-wear evening clothes.

Mainbocher (1890–1976; real name: Main Rousseau Bocher), born in Chicago; originally wanted to be an opera singer. While studying in Paris he became a sketcher for *Harper's Bazar*. He opened his own couture house in Paris, 1922, becoming the first American to succeed as a dressmaker in France. He returned to the U.S. in 1940 and opened a salon in New York in 1941. A master of understatement, he believed in excellent cutting and lavish use of luxury fabrics.

McCardell, Claire (1905–1958), born in Frederick, Maryland; achieved world fame by 1938. She was noted for her "American look" as well as for an artist's sense of color and sculptor's feeling for form.

McQueen, Alexander (b. 1969). Considered an enfant terrible of the fashion world, McQueen was born in London in 1969. He graduated from Central Saint Martin's College of Art and Design in 1992 and quickly gained a reputation as an iconoclast.

Missoni, Rosita and Ottavio (Tai) (Italy). Opening their business in 1953 with four knitting machines, Rosita designed elegant garments while Tai created inventively colored knit patterns.

Mizrahi, Isaac (b. 1961, New York). He studied at the High School of Performing Arts and the Parsons School of Design. His trademark is an unusual, even comic mix of vibrant color with an easy-to-wear, traditional cut.

Montana, Claude (b. 1949, France), began designing papier-mâché jewelry in London in 1971. He stayed in London for a year, then returned to Paris, where he worked for the leather firm MacDouglas and designed for several ready-to-wear firms. In 1972 he established his own business creating clothing with bold, defined shapes.

Mugler, Thierry (b. 1946, France), showed his first collection in Paris in 1971 under the label Café de Paris; by 1973, he was showing clothes under his own name.

Norell, Norman (1900–1972; originally, Norman Levinson), first American elected to Coty Hall of Fame, 1958. He is particularly remembered for precision detail and stunning craftsmanship.

Oldham, Todd (b. 1961, Corpus Christi, Texas) is known for his bold use of color and for serving up kitschy styles with panache.

Patou, Jean (House of): originally creating fashions that were quintessential "Jazz Age," the house hired Karl Lagerfeld in 1960.

Perris, Bernard (b. 1944, France). With early training that included assisting Marc Bohan at Dior, Bernard Perris established a ready-to-wear firm in 1969. His couture-centered designs have a youthful spirit.

Pertegaz, Manuel, born in Aragon, Spain and raised in Barcelona. At age 12 he apprenticed to tailor. He opened own fashion house by 1942 and was well on way to becoming undisputed monarch of Spanish fashion.

Pucci, Emilio (b. 1914, Naples), one of the earliest designers to establish an Italian influence in the postwar era; noted for his printed fabrics.

Quant, Mary (b. 1934, England), a leading figure in the fashion revolution of the sixties, she opened her first boutique in 1955. In 1967, she opened the wildly successful boutique Bazaar on King's Road, 1967; featuring mass-produced miniskirts and fashions that had powerful appeal to the young.

Rabanne, Paco (b. 1934, San Sebastián, Spain), opened his Paris house in 1966. His designs are created through "molding and welding."

Rhodes, Zandra (b. 1940, England), began her career as a textile designer in the mid-sixties, setting up her own printworks with a partner. She began designing clothes using her own fabrics, and by 1969 was working on her own. Zandra Rhodes Limited was established in 1975.

Ricci, Nina (1883–1970), was born in Turin, Italy. At age 13 she was apprenticed to a couturier, and by 21 she was a top stylist. In 1932 she opened her own house, specializing in elegant women's clothes. She was noted for intensely feminine fashions and was one of the first to realize the potential of ready-to-wear. Her principal designer was Jules-François Grahay from 1954–63, followed by Gérard Pipart.

Roehm, Carolyn (b. 1951, United States). She was an assistant designer at Oscar de la Renta, Ltd. from 1975 to 1984, opening Carolyn Roehm Inc. in 1984. Her garments are made in luxurious, embroidered fabrics.

Rykiel, Sonia (b. 1930, France), began her career in 1962 designing her own maternity sweaters. She continued designing after the birth of her child, selling her designs first through her husband's Paris boutique, then through Galeries Lafayette. In 1968, she opened her own store on Paris's Left Bank.

Saint Laurent, Yves (b. 1936, Algeria). Heading the House of Dior after Dior's death in 1957, he opened his own design house in 1962 and Rive Gauche ready-to-wear boutiques in 1966. Saint Laurent popularized blazers, city pants, military jackets, simple dresses divided into Mondrian-inspired blocks of color, and many other styles. In 1963 he became the first living designer to be given a retrospective of his work at New York's Metropolitan Museum of Art.

Scaasi, Arnold (b. 1931, Montreal, Canada). He trained with Charles James, leaving in 1957 to establish his own business. Originally a sketcher and wholesaler, he presented his first ready-to-wear collection in 1960. His specialty is eye-catching evening clothes and spectacular society ball gowns.

Scherrer, Jean-Louis (b. 1936, Paris). His early dance career ended with an injury. He then worked for Christian Dior; after Dior's death, Scherrer opened his own house in 1962. His elegant designs reflect his couture background.

Trigère, Pauline (b. 1912, Paris) came to America to escape the Nazis. She apprenticed at the house of Martial et Armand, then found work on the design staff of Hattie Carnegie. When the Carnegie workrooms closed after the bombing of Pearl Harbor, she sold personal jewelry to finance her own salon. Her designs include foundations, furs, and jewelry, as well as couture-quality ready-to-wear fashions.

Tuffin and Foale. Sally Tuffin (b. 1938, England) and Marion Foale (b. 1939, England) set up a dressmaking business in 1961. Based on Carnaby Street, their designs were aimed at the young ready-to-wear market. The partnership was dissolved in 1972.

Ungaro, Emanuel (b. 1933, France) became a tailor at the age of 14. He first worked for Balenciaga, then Courrèges; in 1965 he opened his own establishment. In the sixties Ungaro was known for his short, structured dresses in bold stripes or plaids and hip-hugger pants. By the seventies he was showing softer colors, shapes, and fabrics. His designs have since become more revealing and sensuous.

Valentino, (1932, Voghera, Italy) has been called the "master of the dress." He studied fashion at the Chambre Syndicale de la Couture. He opened his own design house in Rome in 1959 and his first boutique in Milan in 1969, with many boutiques to follow. Valentino has created gowns for international socialites; Jacqueline Onassis was a client.

Versace, Gianni (1946–1997, Calabria, Italy). Versace's mother was a dressmaker, and he was surrounded by fashion from childhood. He studied architecture but became increasingly involved in his mother's couture business. From rock stars to royalty, his bold, flamboyant designs were worn by men and women in the public eye. His sister, Donatella, carries on the line.

Wang, Vera (b. 1949, New York City). Through her acquaintance with Ralph Lauren, Wang opened a bridal salon and couture business in 1990. Her use of rich fabric, surface decoration, and netting are masterful and dramatic.

001
1950
Dior
Oblique-line
evening
dress

002
1951
Norman Norell
Wasp-waisted dress

003
1951
Jacques Heim
Pants and blouse

004
1951
Mainbocher
Cotton dress

005
1952
Fath
Bell suit

006
1952
Sybil Connolly
Pullover blouse
and at-home
skirt

007
1952
Balenciaga
Plaid suit

008
1953
Hardie Amies
Evening gown

009
1953
*Elspeth
Champcommunal
(for Worth)*
White lace
gown

010
1953
Claire McCardell
"Stringbean"
chemise with
matching
"shortie" jacket

011
1954
Dior
H-line suit

012
1954
Chanel
Jersey suit

013
1954
Balmain
Ball gown

014
1955
Dior
A-line suit

015
1955
Pauline Trigère
Evening dress

016
1955
Pertegaz
Evening coat

017
1956
Balenciaga
Sack-back
day dress

018
1956
Dior
Evening dress

021
1957
*Yves Saint Laurent
(for Dior)*
Trapeze-line
wedding dress

020
1957
Givenchy
Sack dress

019
1956
Charles James
Opera coat

022
1957
Dior
Wool coat

023
1958
Chanel
Jersey suit

024
1958
Cardin
Suit with
blouse-backed
jacket

025
1958
Madame Grès
Evening dress

026
1959
Yves Saint Laurent
Evening suit

027
1959
Irene Galitzine
Sheath dress

028
1959
Givenchy
Gold lamé
dress with
cuffed skirt

029
1960
House of Dior
Silk print suit

030
1960
Jacques Heim
Cotton
evening dress

031
1960
Yves Saint Laurent
Transparent
chiffon dress

032
1961
Irene Galitzine
Crepe jacket
and sheath

033
1961
Jacques Griffe
Linen suit

034
1962
Pierre Balmain
Evening gown

035
1962
Capucci
Chiffon cape-
and-sheath
outfit

036
1962
Courrèges
Nine-tenths
coat

037
1963
Yves Saint Laurent
Organdy outfit

038
1963
Jean Patou
Organdy gown

039
1963
Givenchy
Tweed sport
suit

040
1964
Chanel
Wool suit

041
1964
Larry Aldrich
Unwaisted crepe
dress with stole
(Hat by Halston)

042
1964
Courrèges
Jersey pants
and jacket

043
1964
Yves Saint Laurent
Jersey day dress

044
1965
Pucci
Minidress

045
1965
Courrèges
Wool coat-dress

046
1966
Paco Rabanne
Plastic dress

047
1966
Courrèges
Whipcord and
organza jumpsuit

048
1967
Mary Quant
Wool minidress

049
1967
Rudi Gernreich
Silk dress

050
1967
Bill Blass
Crepe wedding
dress

051
1968
Oscar de la Renta
Organdy
overblouse and
shorts

052
1968
Geoffrey Beene
Coat-dress

053
1968
Anne Fogarty
"Little girl"
dress

054
1969
Courrèges
Dress

055
1969
Pierre Cardin
Wool coat, hooded sweater, and short skirt

056
1969
Yves Saint Laurent
Evening dress

057
1970
Yves Saint Laurent
Lamé dress

058
1970
House of Dior
Crepe-de-chine dress

059
1970
Zandra Rhodes
Quilted satin dress

060
1971
Tuffin and Foale
Checkerboard-print dress and quilted trousers

061
1971
Biba
Wool
pantsuit

062
1971
Chloé
Wraparound
skirt and
shawl

063
1972
Bill Blass
Pleated skirt
and dropped-
waist top

064
1972
Mary Quant
Two-piece
dress

065
1973
Ted Lapidus
Wool pantsuit

066
1973
*Yves
Saint Laurent*
Cardigan, pleated
skirt, and see-
through blouse

068
1974
Loris Azzaro
Mousseline-de-soie
dress

067
1973
Roland Klein
Silk-jersey
dress

069
1974
Laug
Lamé top and
crepe-georgette
skirt

070
1974
Sonia Rykiel
Cape,
sweater, and
skirt

072
1975
Laura Ashley
Pinafore,
skirt, blouse,
and apron

071
1975
John Bates
Duster

073
1976
Halston
Shirtwaist
dress and
jacket

074
1976
Yves Saint Laurent
"Peasant-look"
cape, blouse,
skirt, and turban

075
1977
Givenchy
Dinner dress
with detachable
sleeves

076
1977
*Sisan for
Valentino*
Coordinated
blouse, skirt,
pants, and
scarf

077
1977
Kenzo
"Big Look" shirt
and skirt

078
1978
Courrèges
Jacket, sweater,
shirt, and
trousers

079
1978
Oscar de la Renta
Velvet dress
(brass belt by
Tess Shalom)

080
1978
Yves Saint Laurent
Evening ensemble

081
1979
Thierry Mugler
Jumpsuit

082
1979
Claude Montana
Gabardine trench coat

083
1979
Albert Capraro
Velvet-and-silk evening gown

084
1979
Ralph Lauren
Silk smoking jacket

14   1978–1979

085
1980
*Betty Hanson
and Company*
Shirtwaist dress
and short jacket

086
1980
Missoni
Jacket, hat, and
scarf

087
1980
Claude Montana
Cotton dress

088
1980
Halston
Classic sheath
and box coat

089
1981
Perry Ellis
Tank top with
skirt, petticoats,
knit cap, and
stockings

090
1981
Calvin Klein
Metallic print
dress with
knee-high leather
boots

091
1982
Giorgio Armani
Blouse with
cut-off pants

092
1982
*Marc Bohan for
House of Dior*
Suit

093
1982
Kasper
Silk "tee" shirt
and skirt

094
1983
Bernard Perris
Flannel suit

095
1983
Carolina Herrera
Organza gown

096
1983
*Karl Lagerfeld for
House of Chloé*
Dress with
beads and
sequins

098
1984
Norma Kamali
Fleece top
coat, slacks,
scarf, and
brimmed hat

097
1984
Bill Blass
Evening gown

099
1984
Valentino
Silk sheath

100
1985
Donna Karan
Suede jacket,
wool-jersey
skirt, and
suede boots

101
1985
Gianfranco Ferré
Suede jacket over
slacks

102
1986
Anne Klein
Sweater dress
with patent-
leather belt

103
1986
Adolfo
Dress with a
full-length
zipper

104
1986
Krizia
Ribbed
cashmere-
and-mohair
sweater dress
and coat

105
1987
*Yves
Saint Laurent*
Silk-crepe
evening
gown

106
1987
Geoffrey Beene
Lace
confection

107
1987
Oscar de la Renta
Short dress

108
1988
Emanuel Ungaro
Strapless dress
with dropped
waist and short
skirt

109
1988
Arnold Scaasi
Evening dress
with velvet
bodice and satin
skirt

110
1988
Carolyn Roehm
Wool-crepe
dress with
bolero jacket

111
1988
*Christian
Lacroix*
Wool suit
with mink
facing

112
1989
Bob Mackie
Gown in chiffon
over silk, with a
sequin-studded
jacket

113
1990
Emanuel Ungaro
Lamé evening
gown

114
1990
*Christian
Lacroix*
Patterned silk
ensemble

115
1990
Geoffrey Beene
Silk jacquard
evening
ensemble

116
1991
Oscar de la Renta
Silk-shantung
dress and coat

117
1991
Valentino
Bell-skirted
evening
ensemble

118
1991
Todd Oldham
Patchwork
plaid suit

119
1992
Arnold Scaasi
Polka-dot
strapless
crepe dress

120
1992
Bob Mackie
Velvet-and-taffeta
evening gown

121
1992
Michael Kors
Short strapless
dress and
cardigan

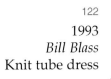

122
1993
Bill Blass
Knit tube dress

123
1993
Adolfo
Polka-dot ensemble

124
1993
*Linda Allard for
Ellen Tracy*
Pin-stripe suit

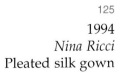

125
1994
Nina Ricci
Pleated silk gown

126
1994
Louis Féraud
Evening gown with
cape-like collar

127
1994
Jean-Louis Scherrer
Minidress ball
gown

128
1995
Vera Wang
Corset-bodice ball gown

129
1995
Thierry Mugler
Miniskirted suit and
vinyl pants

130
1996
Donna Karan
Body-hugging silk
knit tube dress

131
1996
Carolina Herrera
Satin wedding suit

132
1996
Norma Kamali
Panne velvet
lamb-trimmed
ensemble

133
1997
Giorgio Armani
Unstructured great coat
and full-cut pants

134
1997
Isaac Mizrahi
Plunging-neckline
tailored suit

135
1997
Gianni Versace
Slinky silk knit
evening gown

136

1998
John Galliano for Dior
"Scheherazade"
kimono and gown

137

1998
Karl Lagerfeld for Chloé
Sequinned tulle dress

138

1998
*Alexander McQueen
for Givenchy*
Wool coat with gray fox collar

139

1999
Jean Paul Gaultier
Ostrich-trimmed
silk gown with
ostrich fan

140

1999
Ralph Lauren
Cashmere
sweater with
satin ball skirt